Smash.
spring 2002

Published 2002

Editor: Chris Harvey
Cover Design: Space DPS Limited

© International Music Publications Limited
Griffin House 161 Hammersmith Road London W6 8BS England

A Woman's Worth

highest chart position 18
release date 18th March 2002
did you know Alicia Keys dominated the 2002 Grammy Awards, picking up no less than five awards out of the six she was nominated for. Only U2 prevented her from taking the whole half dozen

words and music by

Alicia Augello-Cook and Erika Rose

You could buy me dia - monds, you could buy me
fair - ly, I'll give you all my

pearls, _____ take me on a cruise a - round _ the world. _____ (Ba-
goods; _____ treat you like a real _ wom - an should. _____ (Ba-

A.M. To P.M.

words and music by

Christian Karlsson, Christine Flores and Pontus Winnberg

highest chart position 3
release date 21st January 2002

did you know **Prior to her solo breakthrough R&B singer Milian wrote songs for Jennifer Lopez and provided vocals for Ja Rule's 'Between Me And You' and Missy Elliott and Timbaland protégés Playa**

Some - bo - dy hit the lights, so we can't see it day and

night. Peo - ple get - ting down, that's right, from A. M. to P. M.

Ev - 'ry - bo - dy look - in' like stars, all the chicks and the fel - las in the

bars. All of y'all bump - in' this in your cars, from A. M. to P. M.

day, yeah,————— yeah.— No we don't need to sleep, all night we rock that beat,

so you know what to do, just make your move and make your move.

D.%. al Coda

⊕ *Coda*

N.C.

From A. M. to P. M.

Anything Is Possible

highest chart position 1
release date 25th February 2002

did you know Advance sales of the 'Evergreen'/'Anything Is Possible' double a-side came in at 1.2 million – a figure which proved conservative when the single went on to sell a staggering 1.1 million copies within six days of release

words and music by
Cathy Dennis and Chris Braide

Apple Of My Eye

words and music by
Ed Harcourt

highest chart position 61
release date 4th February 2002
did you know Though Harcourt is routinely compared to the likes of singer-songwriters such as Jeff Buckley, the man himself claims to have previously spent time as a bee-keeper and circus act

1. When you're on your

(1.) own ____ you walk ____ in the rain. ____ You walk a-round the ____
(2.) ____ when I ____ am a-lone. ____ I lose my track of ____

____ house, then walk a-round it ____ a-gain;
____ time, my ideas turn to stone. ____

you pre - tend you're hap - py that you've got it
I pre - tend I'm sad that I'm still so

all. But don't be up - set if you
small. But I'm not up - set 'cos I

fall on your knees and beg like a dog.
fall on my knees and beg like a dog.

I've reached a low, don't you know you're the ap -

D.℘. al Coda

⊕ Coda

I'm sick of this angst; don't need— thanks,— you're the ap - ple of my

eye.

Asleep In The Back

highest chart position 19
release date 11th February 2002
did you know Elbow were first signed to Island, but after they decamped to rural France to record, they endured a collective argument that lasted '16 hours or something'. It resulted in their departure from Island but they were eventually picked up by Richard Branson's V2 label

words and music by

Guy Garvey, Mark Potter, Craig Potter, Richard Jupp and Pete Turner

1. Were you
2. Show your

crushed?
scars.

But I Do Love You

words and music by
Diane Warren

highest chart position 20
release date 4th February 2002
did you know Rimes released her debut album aged just 11 years, and was only 13 when she enjoyed her breakthrough hit in 1996 with 'Blue'. But within a few years she was suing to get out of the childhood contract her parents had signed on her behalf with Curb Records

Verse:

1.4. I don't__ like to_____ be a-lone__ in the night.__
2. I don't__ like to_____ see a sky__ paint-ed gray.__
3. I don't__ like to_____ turn the ra - di - o on__

I don't__ like to_____ hear I'm wrong__ when I'm right.__
I don't__ like when__ noth-ing's go - ing my way.__
just to_____ find I've__ missed my fa - vor-ite song.__

I don't__ like to_____
I don't__ like to_____
I don't__ like to_____

Evergreen

words and music by
**David Kreuger, Jorgen Elofsson
and Per Magnusson**

highest chart position 1
release date **25th February 2002**
did you know **All three finalists for ITV's Pop Idol recorded versions of this double a-side before Will took the crown with one of the biggest telephone polls in history. That consigned versions by opponents Gareth and Darius to the dumper, though Gareth's handlers did get him to re-record a version**

1. Eyes like a
(Verse 2 see block lyric)

sun - rise, like a rain - fall down_ my soul.____ And I

won - der,___ I won - der why you look at me_ like that._ What you're think - ing, what's be - hind._

Verse 2:
Touch, like an angel
Like velvet to my skin
And I wonder
Wonder why you wanna stay the night
What you're dreaming
What's behind
Don't tell me, but it feels like love.

I'm gonna take this moment *etc.*

Fly By

words and music by

**Hallgeir Rustan, Tor Erik Hermansen,
Mikkel Eriksen and Simon Webbe**

highest chart position 6
release date 18th March 2002

did you know Ant of Blue, who used to work as a plumber, dismisses suggestions that they're 'heart-throbs'. "When we go out there and see loads of girls we think, 'Are they here for us or Westlife?'"

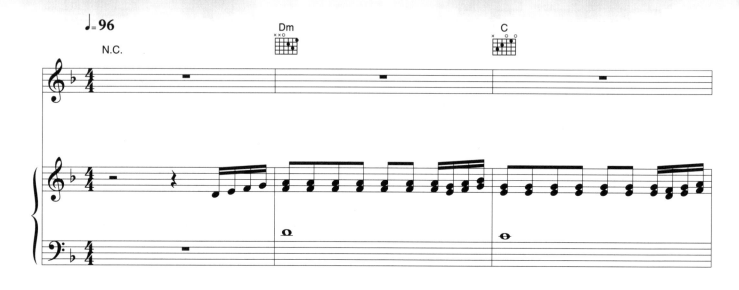

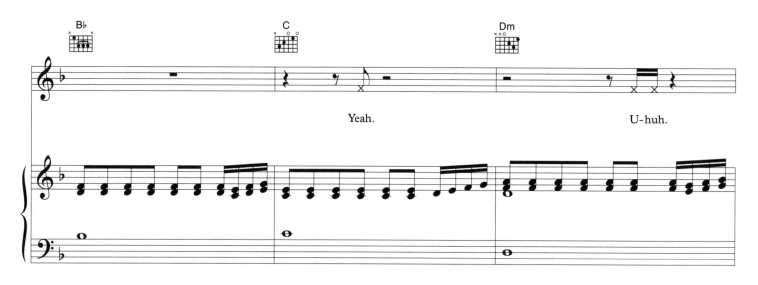

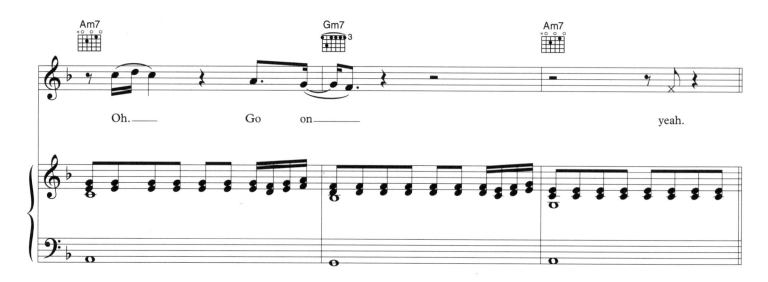

Hey Baby (DJ Otzi)

words and music by
Bruce Channel and Margaret Cobb

highest chart position 3
release date **10th September 2001**

did you know This single followed the classic 'Eurosmash' or 'holiday hit' route to the British charts as exemplified by artists such as Whigfield. In the process it became the biggest Austrian contribution to international charts since Falco ('Amadeus') and Opus ('Live Is Life')

O.K.   Senoritas e cabeleros, say ladies and gentlemen.   Meine damen und herren.   Hey baby!

O.K.   Put your hands up in the air.   Everybody sing now.   Uno, dos, tres, quatro.

Hey, ————————   hey— ba-by.— (Ooh,   ah)   I wan-na know

Freeek!

words and music by

George Michael, Niall Flynn,
James Jackman and Ruadhri Cushnan

highest chart position 7
release date 18th March 2002

did you know In 1985 George Michael received the Ivor Novello Songwriter of the Year Award for his efforts with Wham! He was the youngest ever recipient of the trophy, which was presented by future collaborator Elton John

Hero

words and music by
Enrique Iglesias, Paul Barry and Mark Taylor

highest chart position 1
release date 21st January 2002

did you know Enrique's cultural favourites include Ernest Hemingway, *Pinocchio* and *Bugs Bunny*. He also loves lettuce. Unsurprisingly for a man with the genes of dad Julio, his favourite magazine reading is industry bible *Billboard*

Spoken: Let me be your hero.

Would you

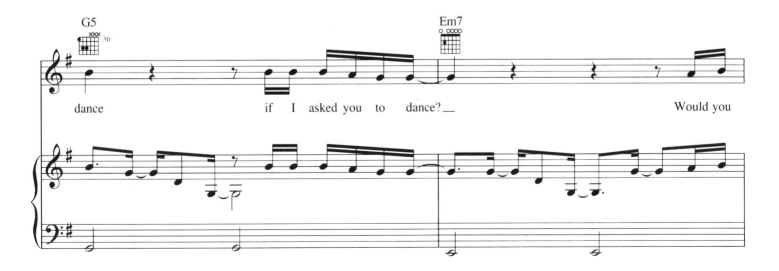

dance   if I asked you to dance?   Would you

Hey Baby (No Doubt)

words and music by

**Gwen Stefani, Tony Kanal,
Tom Dumont and R Price**

highest chart position 2
release date 4th February 2002

did you know The origins of this self-confessed 'loser' band came when Eric Stefani wrote his first song, 'Stick It In The Hole', about a pencil sharpener. He got his sister Gwen to sing along, and voila, a hit combo – albeit one that took a good decade to achieve major success

("Hey ba-by, hey ba-by hey.")

Girls say,— boys say.— ("Hey ba-by, hey ba-by hey.") Hey ba-by, ba-by.—

1. I'm the kind-a girl that hangs with the guys,— like a fly on the wall with my se-cret eyes.—

How Wonderful You Are

words and music by
Gordon Haskell

highest chart position 3
release date **10th December 2001**

did you know **The surprise entrant for the 2001 Christmas number one race, Haskell was a former member of Fleur De Lys, and briefly shared a flat with Jimi Hendrix in the 60s (he lost the tapes of the jam sessions they had together).**

I go out most nights, at-tract-ed by the lights, lis-ten to the jazz at Har-ry's Bar. And I know it won't be long be-fore they play that song, do you

I Think I Love You

highest chart position 10
release date 21st January 2002

words and music by
Tony Romeo

did you know Kaci's first hit came at the age of 14, but by then she'd already been at it for 11 years – begging her father to take her to a local restaurant where she could sing karaoke. Aged nine she recorded her first album – a Christmas themed effort for family and friends. She also appeared in a Disney Christmas special

♩=120

Do you think you love me? Ooh - eee.— Do you think you

love me? Ooh.— Do you think you love me? Ooh - eee.— Do you think you

love me? I think I love you.— 1. I'm

Drums

Verse 3:
Believe me you really don't have to worry
I only wanna make you happy
And if you say go away I will
But I think better still I better stay around and love you
Do you think I have a case?
Let me ask you to your face
Do you think you love me?

I think I love you *etc.*

I Will Always Love You

highest chart position 6
release date 4th March 2002

did you know Waller is, of course, the camera-filling member of the Pop Idol assembly line, famously ejected in favour of Darius after he developed a throat problem. These days he's best mates with Big Brother's Bubble instead

words and music by
Dolly Parton

I'm Not A Girl, Not Yet A Woman

words and music by

Dido Armstrong, Max Martin and Rami Jacoub

highest chart position not released at time of publication

release date 1st April 2002

did you know In 2001 Britney launched her new video game, 'Britney's Dance Beat', on Game Boy Advance – the latest in a list of endorsements that includes Pepsi. Britney features throughout the game as a very strict dance instructor

Slowly ♩ = 76

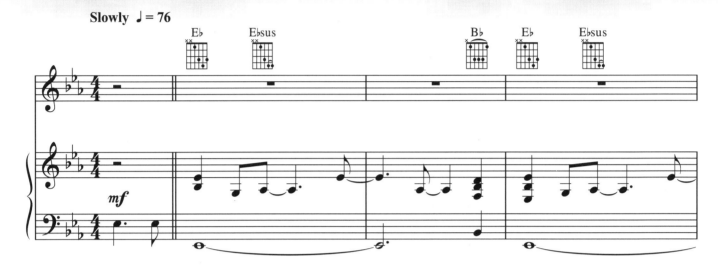

Verse:

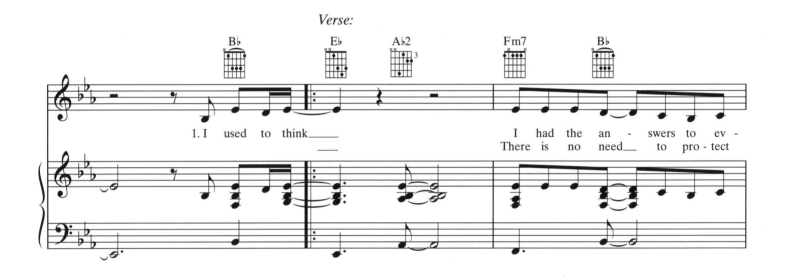

1. I used to think
___

I had the an - swers to ev -
There is no need___ to pro - tect

'ry-thing.
me.

But now I know___
It's time that I___

that

In Your Eyes

highest chart position 3
release date 18th February 2002
did you know Kylie's first TV role actually came when she appeared as a Dutch girl in the wartime Aussie saga *The Sullivans*. In fact *Neighbours* was the sixth soap opera she appeared in (she actually met Jason Donovan in *Skyways*)

words and music by
Kylie Minogue, Richard Stannard, Julian Gallagher and Ashley Howes

1. What on earth am I meant to do? In this crowd-ed place there— is
(Verse 2 see block lyric)

on - ly— you. Was gon-na leave,— now I have to stay.

Verse 2:
Destiny has a funny way
When it comes and takes all your cares away
I can't think of a single thing
Other than what a beautiful state I'm in.

Love Foolosophy

words and music by
Jason Kay and Toby Smith

highest chart position 14
release date 25th February 2002

did you know Jay Kay claims to once have enjoyed the dubious job title of 'kiltmaker', as well as pre-fame spells as a telemarketer. The backing vocals on 'Love Foolosophy' are sung by none other than Beverley Knight

1. Ooh,–

ba - by, ba - by feel these sweet sen - sa - tions, yeah.
2. She shim - mers like a Ca - li - for - nia sun-

A Mind Of It's Own

highest chart position 6
release date 4th February 2002
did you know Victoria Beckham and hubby David make a cameo appearance in *Bend It Like Beckham*, a film documenting a young Indian woman's dreams of playing professional football, which featured look-alikes of the couple

words and music by
**Andrew Frampton, Victoria Beckham
and Steve Kipner**

Love Will Find A Way

words and music by

**Oliver Jacobs, Philip Jacobs, Michael Moore
and Patrick McMahon**

highest chart position not released at time of publication
release date not known at time of publication
did you know Bardot were the Australian forerunners of the Pop Stars format which produced the UK's Hear'Say, with whom they enjoyed a brief duel at the top of the British charts. Tiffany, Belinda, Sophie, Katie and Sally are so popular down under they even have their own magazine

I won-der where you are   I know that

love   will   find_____ a   way_____

There in the distance we meet again
Have you been on your best behavior
We can talk about it later
He's coming for my love
He's the one I'm thinking of
Let me show you what I mean
We'll be living in a dream

More Than A Woman

words and music by
Timothy Mosley and Stephen Garrett

highest chart position 1
release date 7th January 2002
did you know The late Aaliyah was another child prodigy who appeared in concert alongside Gladys Knight aged just 11. At the time of her death in 2001 she had also successfully made the transition to movie roles, including *Romeo Must Die*

1. Pas - sion,_____ in - stant,_____ sweat beads_____ feel me._____ Cu-
(2.) - night,_____ grind - ing,_____ heart - rate's climb - ing._____ You
(Verse 3 see block lyric)

- pid's shot me, my heart - beat's rac - ing._____ Tempt me,_____ try me._____ Feels
- go,_____ I go,_____ 'cause we share pil - lows._____ Taste me,_____ feed me._____ There's

Verse 3:
Constant pleasure
No scale can measure
Secret treasures
Keeps on getting better
Do you wanna fall with me?
We can go to foreign lands
Your hand in my hand
Do you wanna ride with me?
We can be like Bonnie and Clyde
Me by your side.

I'll be more than a lover *etc.*

On The Radio
(Remember The Days)

highest chart position 18
release date 7th January 2002
did you know Prior to making it in the music industry, Furtado held down a number of day jobs including chambermaid and office worker in an alarm company, which gave her an income while she put together her first demo tapes

words and music by
Nelly Furtado

Verse 1:

1. You liked me 'til you heard my s**t on the ra-di-o.

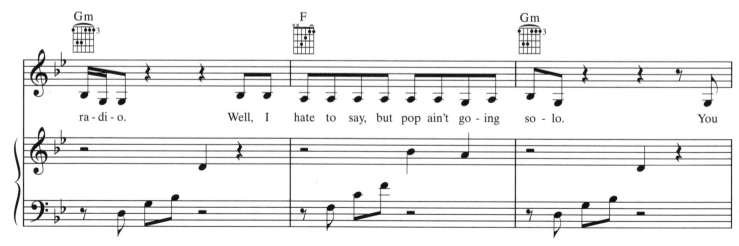

Well, I hate to say, but pop ain't go-ing so-lo. You

To Coda ⊕

day I de - cid - ed to___ stay true to my - self.___

Verse 2:

2. You say your quest is to bring it high - er. Well, I

nev - er seen change with-out a fi - re. But___ from your mouth I have seen___ a lot of

burn - ing,_____ but un - der-neath, I think it's a lot of yearn - ing. Your face,___

People Get Ready

words and music by
Curtis Mayfield

highest chart position has not charted at time of publication

release date 4th March 2002

did you know Cassidy spent several years working as a backing singer before she was struck down by cancer in 1996, just as she began earning recognition. She'd originally put the pain in her hip down to all the ladder work she'd been doing while painting murals in school cafeterias

♩ = 77

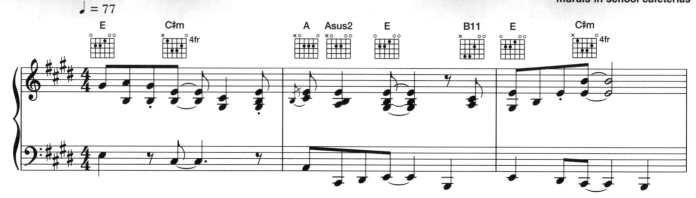

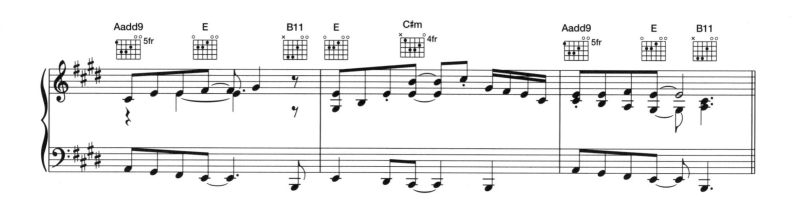

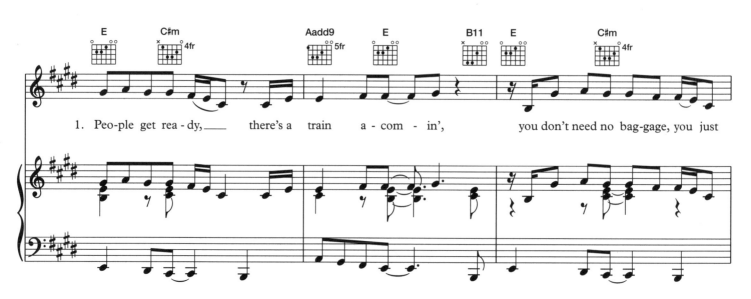

1. Peo-ple get rea-dy,___ there's a train a-com-in', you don't need no bag-gage, you just

Shoulda, Woulda, Coulda

highest chart position 10
release date 18th February 2002
did you know The rising R&B star claims that there are two very important things she always takes on tour with her – vitamin pills, to keep her energy levels up, and lipgloss

words and music by
Beverley Knight and Craig Wiseman

1. Peo-ple say that to-geth-er we were both sides
2. I could see in the dis-tance all the dreams that were
(Verse 3 see block lyric)

of the same coin,
near to me.

that we would shine like Ve - nus in a clear night
And ev - 'ry choice I had to make left you

Verse 3:
People ask how it feels to live the kind of life others dream about
I tell them everybody gotta face their highs and their lows
And in my life there's a love that I put aside, 'cause I was busy loving something else
So for every little thing you hold on to, you've got to let something else go.

And how I wish *etc.*

Silent To The Dark

highest chart position 23
release date 4th March 2002
did you know Prior to forming the Electric Soft Parade,
brothers Alex and Tom had already
released three self-financed albums
as Feltro Media

words and music by
Tom White

Small cost, it pays—— to be a - lone.——

Small talk on the ra - di - o,—— it seems—— I am go - ing no - where to-

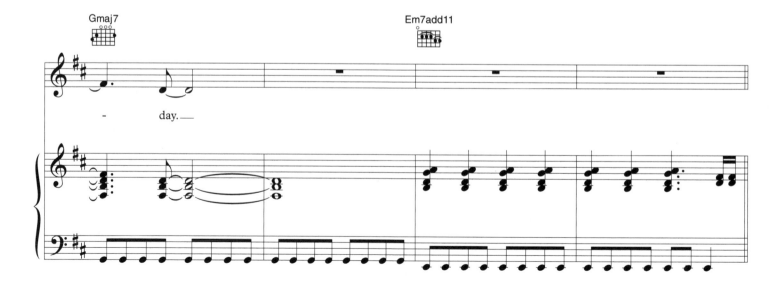

- day.——

Sugar For The Soul

words and music by
Ali Thomson and Peter Vettese

highest chart position 32
release date 11th March 2002

did you know Prior to launching his pop career, Balsamo's face was already easily recognised – having been plastered on billboards throughout London in his guise as Jesus in Andrew Lloyd Webber's production of *Jesus Christ Superstar*. Nevertheless, he describes himself as "more of a pints man than a tights man"

1. Got a feel-ing there's some-thing chang-ing, there's a new star
2. I've found some-one that goes much deep-er, al-ways keeps me

May It Be

words and music by

Enya, Nicky Ryan and Roma Ryan

highest chart position 50
release date 28th January 2002

did you know After leaving Clannad, Eithne Ni Bhraonain (aka Enya) got a break when her lyricist partner Roma Ryan sent a tape of her music to David Puttnam, who featured her on the score to *The Frog Prince*

Slowly and freely ♩ = 76

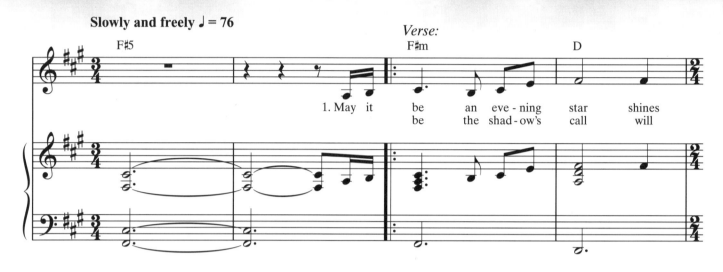

1. May it be an eve-ning star shines
   be the shad-ow's call shines will

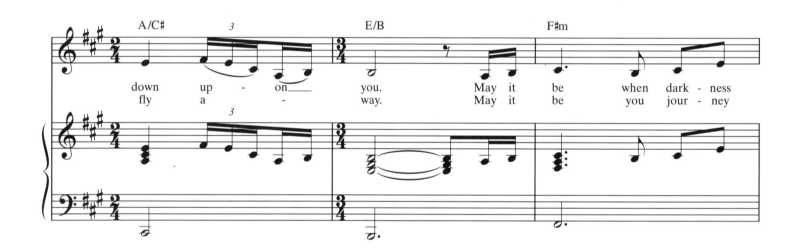

down up-on you. May it be when dark-ness
fly a-way. May it be when you jour-ney

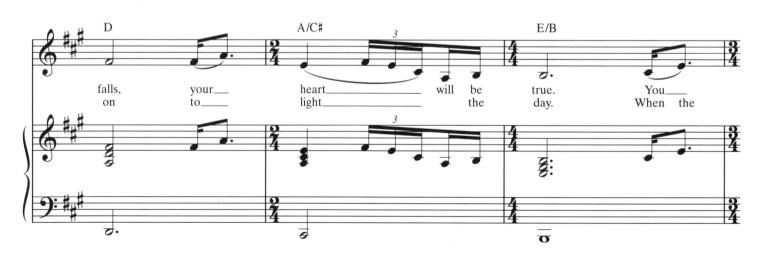

falls, your heart will be true. You
on to light the day. When the

prom - ise lives_____ with - in you

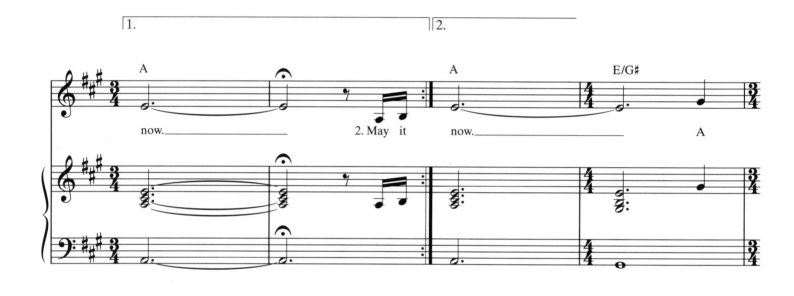

now._____

2. May it now._____ A

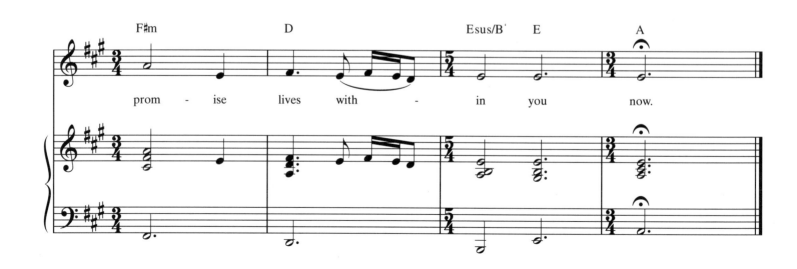

prom - ise lives with - in you now.

Point Of View

words and music by

**Monica Bragato, Alfredo Comazzetto,
Thomas Croquet, Christian Mazzalai,
Laurent Mazzalai and Frederic Moulin**

highest chart position 3
release date 18th February 2002

did you know Italian dance act DB Boulevard feature the voice of Venetian Moony. And while the group fought it out with Victoria Beckham for the number one spot (only for both to be beaten by Enrique Iglesias), Moony revealed that she was good friends with Spiller, who beat Mrs Beckham to the number one spot back in 2000 with 'Groovejet'

Don't have a cent,— will I pay my rent?—

Watching Xanadu

words and music by
Colin MacIntyre

highest chart position 36
release date 21st January 2002
did you know Mull Historical Society is to all intents and purposes Colin MacIntyre, a native of the western Scottish isle, who mixed native folk influences with the likes of the Beatles and Clash. But before he could become a full-time musician he endured a spell working for BT on their directory enquiries service

1. She said some-one else is hap-py, some-one else is care-
2. She said put the world be-tween us, ce-le-brate and pack

- free, some-one else is here and now. Oh,
up, op-en up our eyes and jump. Oh,

World Of Our Own

words and music by
Steve Mac and Wayne Hector

highest chart position 1
release date 18th February 2002
did you know This was the Irish boy band's 10th number one single. However, it dropped straight out of the Top Five the next week, to be replaced by Pop Idol Will Young singing 'Evergreen', one of their former hits

all of the time I'm look-ing for some-thing new. What am I do-ing with-out__ you?

1.

What am I do-ing with-out__ you?__

2. Well I guess I'm

2.

Well it's feel-ing right__ now so let's do it right__ now.

all of the time I'm look - ing for some - thing new. World of__ our own.____

new. What am I do - ing with - out__ you.____

Verse 2:
Well I guess I'm ready
For settling down
And fooling around is over
And I swear that it's true
No buts or maybe's
When I'm falling down
There's always someone saves me
And girl it's you
Funny how life can
Be so surprising
I'm just realising what you do.

We got a little world of our own   *etc.*

8858A PVG

Black Coffee - Bob The Builder – Can't Fight The Moonlight – Charlie's Angels – Could I Have This Kiss Forever – Dancing In The Moonlight – Groovejet (If This Ain't Love) – Heartbreak Hotel – Holler – I Believe – I Put A Spell On You – I Turn To You – In Demand – Kids – Lucky – Music – My Love – Natural – On A Night Like This – On The Radio – Ordinary World – Overload – Please Don't Turn Me On – She Bangs – Should I Stay – The Way You Make Me Feel – This I Promise You – Unforgivable Sinner – Walking Away – What Makes A Man – Why Does My Heart Feel So Bad? – You Need Love Like I Do (Dont You)

9083A PVG

Always Come Back To Your Love – Back Here – Chase The Sun – Chemistry – Dance With Me – Don't Tell Me – Falling – He Don't Love You – He Loves You Not – Jaded – I Can't Deny It – I Need You – I'm Like A Bird – If That Were Me – Inner Smile – Let Love Be Your Energy – Love Don't Cost A Thing – Lovin' Each Day – My Girl – Never Had A Dream Come True – New Year – No More – Nobody Wants To Be Lonely – Out Of Reach – Rendezvous – Supreme – Teenage Dirtbag – Think About Me – Too Busy Thinking 'Bout My Baby – Uptown Girl – What It Feels Like For A Girl – Whole Again – You Make Me Sick

9320A PVG

All For You – Angel – Boss Of Me – Crystal – Electric Avenue – Eternal Flame – Eternity – Here With Me – Here And Now – Hunter – I Don't Want A Lover – Irresistible – It Wasn't Me – It's Raining Men – Lady Marmalade – Little L – A Little Respect – Loaded – Made For Lovin' You – Over The Rainbow – Run For Cover – Scream If You Wanna Go Faster – Someone To Call My Lover – Still On Your Side – Take Me Home – Take My Breath Away – Thank You – There You'll Be – Too Close – Turn Off The Light – Twentyfourseven – The Way To Your Love

9531A PVG

All The Way To Reno (You're Gonna Be A Star) – All You Want – Brown Skin – Can't Get You Out Of My Head – Drowning – Emergency 72 – Fallin' – Feeling Good – Gone – Handbags And Gladrags – Have You Ever – I Want Love – If You Come Back – Lullaby – Luv Me, Luv Me – Murder On The Dancefloor – Only Time – Paid My Dues – Queen Of My Heart – The Road To Mandalay – Smooth Criminal – Somethin' Stupid – That Day – This Train Don't Stop There Anymore – Walking On Sunshine – What If – Words Are Not Enough – You Are – You Give Me Something – You Rock My World

9524A Easy Piano

Can We Fix It? – Can't Fight The Moonlight – Dancing In The Moonlight – Eternal Flame – Eternity – Here And Now – Here With Me – Holler – Nelly Furtado – Inner Smile – It's Raining Men –,It Wasn't Me – Kids – Lady Marmalade – Love Don't Cost A Thing – Lovin' Each Day – Music – Never Had A Dream Come True – On The Radio– Out Of Reach – Over The Rainbow – Overload – Take Me Home – Teenage Dirtbag – Thank You – There You'll Be – Uptown Girl – Walking Away – The Way To Your Love – Whole Again

A comprehensive collection of pop hits

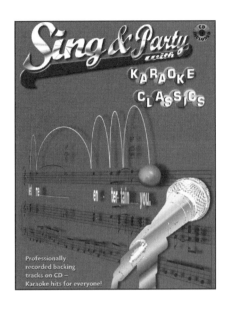

Karaoke Classics
9696A   PVG/CD   ISBN: 1-84328-202-X

Back For Good - Delilah - Hey Baby - I Will
Always Love You - I Will Survive - Let Me
Entertain You - Reach - New York, New York -
Summer Nights - Wild Thing

Party Hits
9499A   PVG/CD   ISBN: 1-84328-097-8

Come On Eileen - Dancing Queen - Groove Is In
The Heart - Hi Ho Silver Lining - Holiday - House
Of Fun - The Loco-Motion - Love Shack - Staying
Alive - Walking On Sunshine

Disco
9493A   PVG/CD   ISBN: 1-84328-091-4

I Feel Love - I Will Survive - I'm So Excited - Lady
Marmalade - Le Freak - Never Can Say Goodbye
- On The Radio - Relight My - Fire - YMCA - You
Sexy Thing

YOU'RE THE VOICE

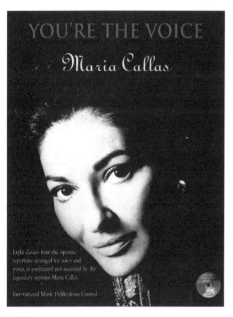

8861A PV/CD

Casta Diva from Norma - Vissi D'arte from Tosca - Un Bel Di Vedremo from Madam Butterfly - Addio, Del Passato from La Traviata - J'ai Perdu Mon Eurydice from Orphee Et Eurydice - Les Tringles Des Sistres Tintaient from Carmen - Porgi Amor from Le Nozze Di Figaro - Ave Maria from Otello

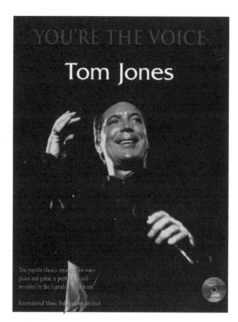

8860A PVG/CD

Delilah - Green Green Grass Of Home - Help Yourself - I'll Never Fall In Love Again - It's Not Unusual - Mama Told Me Not To Come - Sexbomb Thunderball - What's New Pussycat - You Can Leave Your Hat On

9297A PVG/CD

Beauty And The Beast - Because You Loved Me - Falling Into You - The First Time Ever I Saw Your Face - It's All Coming Back To Me Now - Misled - My Heart Will Go On - The Power Of Love - Think Twice - When I Fall In Love

9349A PVG/CD

Chain Of Fools - A Deeper Love Do Right Woman, Do Right Man - I Knew You Were Waiting (For Me) - I Never Loved A Man (The Way I Loved You) I Say A Little Prayer - Respect - Think Who's Zooming Who - (You Make Me Feel Like) A Natural Woman

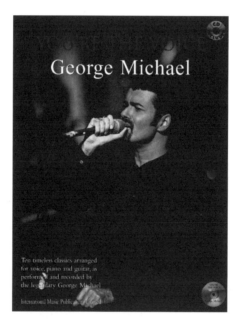

9007A PVG/CD

Careless Whisper - A Different Corner Faith - Father Figure - Freedom '90 I'm Your Man - I Knew You Were Waiting (For Me) - Jesus To A Child Older - Outside

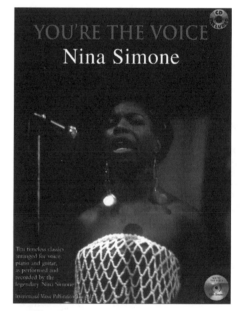

9606A PVG/CD

Don't Let Me Be Misunderstood - Feeling Good - I Loves You Porgy - I Put A Spell On You - Love Me Or Leave Me - Mood Indigo - My Baby Just Cares For Me Ne Me Quitte Pas (If You Go Away) - Nobody Knows You When You're Down And Out - Take Me To The Water

The outstanding new vocal series from IMP

CD contains full backings for each song,
professionally arranged to recreate the sounds of the original recording